Breamore Yesterday and Today

by Anthony Light
and Gerald Ponting

Charlewood Press

The text of this book is a revised and extended version of that in
Breamore - a Short History and Guide
by the same authors, published in 1994

Published by Charlewood Press
7, Weavers Place, Chandler's Ford, SO53 1TU

http://home.clara.net/gponting/index-page10.html

British Library
Cataloguing in Publication Data
A catalogue record for this book is available from the British Library

ISBN 0 9533955 5 3

Typesetting, layout and design by the authors using
Microsoft Word, Corel PhotoPaint and Serif PagePlus

Printed by Hobbs the Printers
Totton, Hants

CONTENTS

BACK COVER: Breamore Mill, from a print by
J. Sigrist, 1792 *(see page 44)*.

COVER ILLUSTRATION: Green's Farm, at the junction of the main road and the lane to Woodgreen; an engraving from a painting by Frederick Albert Slocombe, dating from the second half of the 19th century.

Copyright © Reproduced with permission from the Thomas Ross Collection – hand coloured prints available at www.intaglio-fine-art.com

BELOW: the same spot in 2005.

A map of the historical Parish of Breamore, as it existed until late in the 19th century. Today, the boundaries are very similar, although both North and South Charford are included, while lands to the east of the river are now part of Woodgreen.

SEVERAL OF THE BUILDINGS DESCRIBED AND ILLUSTRATED IN THIS BOOK ARE PRIVATE DWELLINGS – PLEASE RESPECT THE PRIVACY OF THE OCCUPANTS.

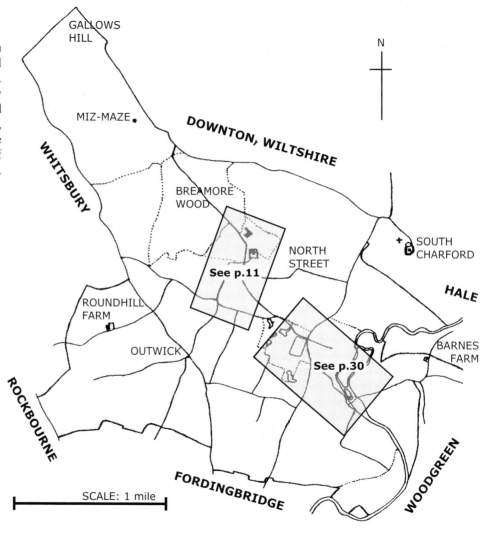

GALLOWS HILL

MIZ-MAZE

N

DOWNTON, WILTSHIRE

WHITSBURY

BREAMORE WOOD

NORTH STREET

See p.11

SOUTH CHARFORD

HALE

ROUNDHILL FARM

OUTWICK

See p.30

BARNES FARM

ROCKBOURNE

SCALE: 1 mile

FORDINGBRIDGE

WOODGREEN

4

BREAMORE - Historical Outline

Breamore is a largely unspoilt Hampshire village situated in the valley of the River Avon, just south of the Wiltshire border. The name is always pronounced 'BREMMER'. Unlike many villages, it is free of modern suburban–style development and is now protected by Conservation Area status.

The Giant's Grave long barrow is a mound, now covered with bushes, on the chalk downs not far from the Miz-Maze.

Within the parish boundary, there are low-lying meadows, large areas of fertile arable land, woodland and chalk downland. The village housing is somewhat scattered – some cottages along the main Salisbury-Bournemouth road, and others near the Mill, around the edge of the village 'common' (known as 'The Marsh') and in Upper Street. There are also a number of outlying farms and houses, as well as the nearby hamlet of Outwick.

People have inhabited the area from early times. Numerous worked flints of the Neolithic and Bronze Ages, as well as of the earlier Mesolithic period, have been recovered over much of the area. More substantial remains from the Neolithic and Bronze Ages may be seen on the chalk downs beyond Breamore Wood. These include early burial sites such as the long-barrow known as the 'Giant's Grave', and a number of round-barrows. The north-western boundary of the parish follows Grim's Ditch, part of the extensive ditch system that divided up the Bronze Age downland landscape. Recent archaeological work has revealed traces of Bronze Age round barrows in the valley at North Street.

Barbed and tanged flint Bronze Age arrowhead found in a field at Roundhill, Breamore (cm scale)

By the Iron Age, farms and hamlets had been established throughout the area. It is clear that the countryside was already as extensively

The Roman coin hoard, discovered in 1996, as displayed in Breamore House

The 6th-century 'bucket' found near the Mill

farmed and managed as it was to be in later times. Undoubtedly many of these Celtic settlements continued in use into the Roman period. Roman pottery has been recovered in considerable quantities from at least five occupation sites. Although several Roman villas are known from the surrounding countryside (including that at Rockbourne, which is open to the public), there is little evidence to suggest that the local settlements acquired stone buildings or any great degree of sophistication. In 1996 a hoard of over 4600 Roman coins of the late 3rd century was found in a field near North Street, buried in a pottery jar *(see other publications, page 48)*.

Charford, in the north of the parish, is said to derive its name from 'Cerdic's Ford'. According to the Anglo-Saxon Chronicle, the battle of Cerdic's Ford took place in 519 AD. The native Britons, no doubt still clinging to vestiges of Romano-British culture, were reputedly defeated by the Anglo-Saxon settlers led by Cerdic. The Saxon victory eventually resulted in the establishment of the Kingdom of Wessex. Archaeological studies have revealed extensive evidence of occupation from the Saxon period in various parts of the village.

In 1999 a metal-detectorist discovered a finely-decorated bronze 'bucket' or drinking vessel in a field near Breamore Mill. The style showed that it had been imported from the region of present-day Syria. This led to an intensive investigation in 2001 by the archaeologists of Channel 4's *Time Team* – and several burials with further high-status grave goods, including more 'buckets', were unearthed. Subsequent finds suggest that there may be a further cemetery in the village, with an occupation site nearby.

The settlement of 'Brumore', the forerunner of modern Breamore, probably originated in the 8th or 9th centuries A.D. If there was a nucleated settlement at this time, which is uncertain, it is likely to have been near the church or along present-day North Street. The church was built either at the end of the 10th century or early in the 11th. It was a royal foundation and stood within a large enclosure; a royal House or Palace may have existed to the west of the church.

At the time of the Domesday Survey in 1086, the village was still small, apparently consisting of only twelve households. Gradually the settlement spread southwards and eastwards with new groups of houses around the Marsh and the Mill – by 1300 there seem to have been about fifty dwellings. As the population grew, so there was an increase in arable land taken from the hitherto uncultivated 'waste'.

In the midst of this expansion, the Priory was founded on the west bank of the Avon in about 1130. Over the next two centuries the Prior and Canons acquired about half of the houses and land in the village, much of it on the more recently settled southern side. The remainder was held by the de Redvers family, who were Lords of the Manor of Breamore, as well as Earls of Devon; they built a substantial manor-house near the church.

Adjoining the manor-house was the Manor Farm, with a large stock of cattle, sheep and pigs. The Reeve based there was responsible for managing extensive areas of arable, meadow and downland. Much of the Priory estate was run from monastic farms, known as granges, at Barnes and at Roundhill. (These later became Barnes Farm at Woodgreen and Roundhill Farm on the lane to Whitsbury.)

The Breamore entry in Domesday Book, 1086 (as typeset in 1783). It records that the village was a royal manor held by Saxon kings and by William I. There were four 'villagers' and eight 'small-holders', with four ploughs and 82 acres of meadow.
Reproduced by permission of Phillimore & Co (see page 48)

The ruined Priory was used as a 'quarry' for many years. This carved stone became part of the foundations of a barn near Breamore School and was rediscovered after the barn collapsed in the 1980s.

An example of early-17th-century timber-framing with later brick infill

The outbreak of the Black Death in the middle of the 14th century had disastrous effects throughout the country. Further outbreaks during the 15th century resulted in the breakdown of long-established social conventions. In Breamore, as elsewhere, the manorial system began to collapse. The manor-house fell into disrepair and the Priory's income was significantly depleted. Much of the farmland was leased to tenant farmers for monetary rents, rather than for work-services as in feudal times.

Henry VIII's dissolution of the monasteries had its effects in Breamore. The Priory was forced to close on 5th July 1536 and its property was granted to new owners. By 1580, William Dodington, Auditor of the Tower Mint, had purchased much of the village, including the former Priory property. He soon built the splendid new Elizabethan-style manor-house which survives today, with a few alterations and additions, as Breamore House.

The 16th century finally saw the end of the medieval way of life. A new breed of yeoman farmers emerged, with much greater security of tenure than previously, and more incentive to farm at a profit. The old unenclosed open fields were beginning to be hedged and fenced, resulting in the patchwork of small fields long considered to be 'typical English countryside'. The housing stock remained largely medieval in style until near the end of the 16th century when the 'great Tudor rebuild' began. Some of the cottages that we see in Breamore today are of this period, although most date from the first few decades of the following century.

The turmoil of the Civil War does not appear to have affected Breamore directly, although the Dodingtons are known to have been active supporters of Parliament. With the death of Lady Anne Brooke (née Dodington) in 1691, ownership of Breamore passed to the Brooke family of Warwick Castle. In 1748 the House and estates were purchased by Sir Edward Hulse. Breamore House has remained the home of the Hulse family ever since, and for much of this time, the bulk of the village has constituted their estate.

Over the past two-and-a-half centuries there have, of course, been many changes to village life, some more radical than others. Many old cottages have survived, others have inevitably needed replacing, while additional estate-workers' cottages were built in Victorian times. The countryside has evolved to suit changing fashions in agriculture, particularly since the Second World War. Fields have been enlarged to accommodate modern machinery; the 17th-century system of water-meadow irrigation has fallen out of use within the past forty years; and the Downs no longer echo to the bleating of large flocks of sheep.

In the years after the Second World War, almost every dwelling in the village was still occupied by a farmer, smallholder or estate-worker, many of whose parents and grandparents had worked the same lands. In contrast, few of today's occupants are involved in farming and many are new to the village. The railway has come and gone, the horse and cart has disappeared, while the general availability of the motor car has perhaps done more to change the old way of life than any other single factor.

Despite all of these changes, the village has retained much of its 'olde worlde' atmosphere. Here, more than in most villages, the visitor, with a little imagination, should be able to visualise the past and to recognise some of the historical developments that have produced the community we see today. We hope that this book – and other publications that we recommend *(see page 48)* – will assist in this process.

Tractor at work near the Miz-Maze in the mid-1980s. This arable field, like many others on the downs, had once been open chalk grassland.

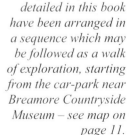

The points of interest detailed in this book have been arranged in a sequence which may be followed as a walk of exploration, starting from the car-park near Breamore Countryside Museum – see map on page 11.

One of the most popular exhibits in the Museum - a reconstruction of the interior of a farm labourer's cottage as it might have looked during much of the first half of the 20th century

For details of Museum opening times see page 12. Special events are held on various dates through the summer season.

THE COUNTRYSIDE MUSEUM

In the 18th century, the Breamore House kitchen garden was situated about 200 yards north-east of the house. Early in the 19th century, this area was cleared and incorporated into the newly expanded park.

The Countryside Museum is set within the walls of the new kitchen garden, built between 1799 and 1802, some 300 yards to the south of the House. The walled gardens of country houses, so important in the Victorian period, had become uneconomic by the middle of the 20th century. At Breamore, the site proved ideal for the construction of the Museum in 1971.

There is much on display in the Museum to fascinate anyone with an interest in rural history. A wide range of tools, machinery and household items helps to depict the all-but-vanished rural life of earlier generations. There are implements relating to all aspects of farm work, as well as horse-drawn machinery, wagons, steam engines and tractors. Special exhibits recreate workshops of the blacksmith, wheelwright, saddler and boot-maker amongst others, while a 'village street' includes a schoolroom, garage and grocery shop. The shelves of the latter are stocked with many hundreds of once familiar household items, which will stir the memories of older visitors in particular.

The reconstruction of a farmworker's cottage is evocative to everyone who experienced life before electricity, when the smell of the paraffin lamp pervaded the room. A wattle-and-daub panel on display nearby was removed from a cottage during renovation in the mid-1980s. (This cottage, near the school, was formerly the Wellington Arms - *see page 41*.) Most of the cottages in the village were originally constructed of timber frames, infilled with such panels.

Leaving the Countryside Museum, follow the signs and walk up through the open parkland to Breamore House.

An unusual feature of the museum is a brick maze, which was laid out in 1983. Its design, based on the shape of inter-locking five-bar gates, was the winning entry in a Sunday Times Magazine competition.

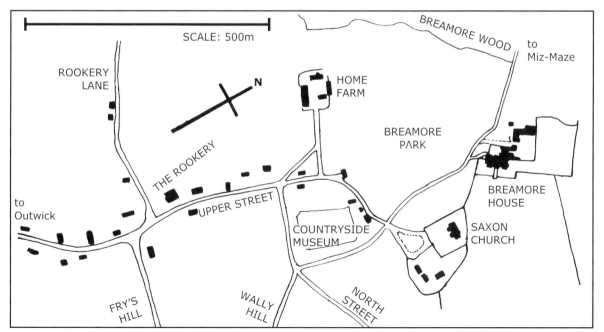

SCALE: 500m

Plan of the upper part of Breamore village

BREAMORE HOUSE

'A View of Sir Edward Hulse's Breamore Hants'
This print by J. Sigrist, dating from 1792, is the earliest known illustration of the house.
The Saxon church is shown among the trees on the left.
In the modern photograph *opposite*, the Victorian water tower is seen to the left of the House.

Built between 1580 and 1583 by William Dodington, Auditor of the Tower Mint, Breamore House still retains much of its external Elizabethan appearance. The body of the house was, at that time, only one room in width, giving the State Rooms on the first floor a light and airy feel with large windows to both back and front. Several rooms were added at the rear in the 18th and 19th centuries. The main entrance has always been from the rear, so it is now further back than its original position. Also, the courtyard was much lower than today, so that the door into the Hall was formerly approached via at least 12 steps.

An open Gallery ran the entire length of the body of the house on the 'attic' floor. The kitchens and other working rooms were on the first floor of the back wing, with cellars under the main block that were entered below the steps leading up to the hall.

The Tudor gardens in front of the house were approached from the terrace. They were remodelled and extended by the Brooke family in the 1660s, but were swept away in the mid-18th century by the second Sir Edward Hulse.

On pages 13-17, we outline the stories of the two families who have occupied Breamore House.

12

Breamore House and the Countryside Museum are open to the public in the afternoons during the summer season. Guides give an informative tour of many of the rooms. A full-colour Guide-Book is available (see page 48). Opening days and times vary from month to month. For details and prices phone 01725 512468 or 512233; collect a leaflet from a local Tourist Information Centre; or see www.hants.gov.uk/discover/places/breamorehouse.html.

Shield from the Dodington coat of arms: 'Argent. Three hunting horns sable with their strings gules'

The Dodington Family of Breamore House

The Dodington family was afflicted by a succession of tragedies. After a long legal battle with a neighbouring landowner, William Dodington committed suicide in January 1600 by jumping from the tower of St Sepulchre's church near his London home.

Part of his suicide note read: '... *John Bulkeley and his fellows by perjury … have brought me to this … ... surely after they had thus slandered me, every day that I lived was to me an hundred deaths, which caused me to choose to die with Infamy, than to live with Infamy and Torment …'*.

He was succeeded by his son, also William, who was knighted by James I on his Coronation Day in 1603. None of Sir William's sons survived into old age; one of them, Henry, still in his late twenties, was hanged for the murder of his mother in 1629. A contemporary account stated:

'One Dodington, being reprehended for some disorderly courses by his mother, drew his sword and ran her twice through, and afterwards, she being dead, gave her many wounds; and had slain his sister at the same time, had he not been prevented.'

One account states that he was hanged '... *in sight of the house where he was untimely born'*. It was customary at the time to erect a gallows near to the site of a murder.

Sir William considered that the suicide of his father, the murder of his wife and the execution of his son were 'punishment' for his father having 'profited from the Church's misfortunes' in purchasing lands which had belonged to the dissolved monasteries. He attempted to atone for this by financial support of the Church and by undertaking many public duties, including Justice of the Peace and Sheriff of Hampshire.

The family fortunes never recovered after the suicide and murder. The Dodington male line died out in 1656. Sir William's granddaughter Anne married Robert, Lord Brooke of Warwick Castle. The tragedies continued even then – all six of their sons died in childhood.

Between 1694 and 1710 the Brookes leased Breamore House to the 5th Lord Arundel, while his home at Wardour Castle in Wiltshire was being rebuilt. For much of the next forty years, Breamore House was often largely unoccupied. In 1748 the house and estates were sold to Sir Edward Hulse. His descendants have lived here ever since (see pages 16-17).

There is a superstition concerning the portrait of Christian Dodington *(left)*, wife of the first William, which hangs in the Great Hall – anyone who moves it is risking sudden death soon afterwards!

Gallows Hill is on the downs, at the northernmost extremity of the parish. It is likely to have been the site of medieval executions, possibly even that of Henry Dodington. Only trees mark the spot today.

The Hulse Family of Breamore House

The Hulse coat of arms

Edward Hulse, a descendant of an old Cheshire family, was King William III's Court Physician. His son, also Edward (1682-1759), carried on the family tradition, becoming Physician in Ordinary to Queen Anne and then to King George I. Under George II, he became First Physician to the royal family. He was knighted by the king in 1739 for saving the life of the Prince of Wales.

Nine years after becoming a baronet, Sir Edward bought the Breamore Estates from Lord Brooke of Warwick Castle. He never actually lived at Breamore, his home being at Baldings near Dartford in Kent, but gave the property to his eldest son, also Sir Edward (1715-1800).

At the time of the purchase in 1748, Breamore House was in urgent need of repair, having been badly neglected for some time. Sir Edward (2nd Baronet) set about restoring the buildings and modernising them internally. He moved here permanently in 1760. He also had the old formal gardens in front of the House grassed over and incorporated into the Park. A new and more fashionable walled garden, which still largely survives, was constructed on the north side. Account books of the time show that Sir Edward introduced greenhouses and hotbeds with numerous exotic plants.

His descendants have continued to live at Breamore. Over the years, and particularly in the early part of the 19th century, the Park was further extended and many specimen trees were planted, particularly by Sir Charles Hulse (4th Baronet, 1771-1854). Some of these may still be seen.

Breamore House contains a fine selection of art-works, some of them quite unexpected, such as a series of Mexican ethnological paintings. The collection is the result both of purchase by successive members of the family and of significant acquisitions through marriage in several generations.

The House was requisitioned by the British Army soon after the outbreak of the Second World War. Towards the end of 1943, American forces replaced the British. In the run-up to D-Day, General Paton was briefly based here. Furniture and art treasures were removed during the military occupation, though the Dodington portrait remained in place, no-one wanting to risk falling foul of the 'curse'!

Today, Breamore House remains the home of the Hulse family.

Leaving Breamore House, many visitors go next to the nearby Saxon Church (see page 20). However, the bridleway which leads up the edge of the park by the House passes through Breamore Wood and leads to the ancient Miz-Maze (see page 18). This is a walk of about a mile each way.
The booklet 'A Walk to Breamore Miz-Maze' (see page 48) describes the walk and the maze in full.

A portrait by Francis Coates of Sir Edward Hulse, Second Baronet (1715-1800). He was the first member of the family to live in Breamore House.

THE MIZ-MAZE

The Miz-Maze as illustrated by Heywood Sumner in 1913. The wood which surrounds the maze is clearly a relatively modern development.

The Miz-Maze is situated on a downland hilltop beyond Breamore Wood. The Wood was once the medieval deer-park of the Earls of Devon, who then owned Breamore. Part of the old boundary bank and ditch may still be seen at the northern end of the woods where the downland begins. For centuries the downs were used as sheep pasture for the Manor Farm and the Priory Farm at Roundhill, but today most of the land is devoted to arable crops.

The Miz-Maze is a turf-cut labyrinth (with no blind endings) about 84 feet in diameter. The continuous grassy path, defined by chalk-cut 'ditches' is formed of eleven concentric rings, each about 2ft 6ins in width. It leads to a central mound which has a diameter of 17 feet. The pattern of the maze is identical to that of the much smaller design set out in tiles on the floor of Chartres Cathedral. Countless similar mazes once existed on village greens throughout the country. The Breamore maze and another on St. Catherine's Hill, Winchester, are two of only eight remaining.

The origins and purpose of the maze are obscure, although it is almost certainly of medieval date, as suggested by the considerable quantities of medieval pottery recovered nearby. The fragments were concentrated within a few yards of the north-east edge of the Miz-Maze, and might suggest that feasting accompanied whatever rituals took place here.

By the 17th century, Breamore Miz-Maze was apparently overgrown and largely forgotten. However, its outlines must still have been visible in 1783, when Sir Edward Hulse (2nd Baronet) ordered it to be re-cut. Since that time it has been regularly maintained by the Breamore Estate. It is now a Scheduled Ancient Monument and is fenced to protect it from wear and tear from large numbers of visitors.

This aerial photograph was taken from an Optica aircraft in 1989. The maze appears very clearly defined, as it had recently been re-cut and the chalk 'ditches' showed up very clearly in the sunshine. (Picture by Henry Wills, courtesy of *Salisbury Journal*)

Returning from Breamore House or from a walk to the Miz-Maze, turn left after leaving Breamore Park. The entrance to the churchyard is a short distance ahead.

ST MARY'S CHURCH

The church as it may have appeared when first built, with an extra western chamber, a taller tower and original windows

The church before removal of the plaster coating in 1897

The Church of St Mary, Breamore was built in about 1000 A.D. as the mother church of a Minster parish that encompassed other nearby villages. Much of the original fabric survives and the church today is probably the finest existing example of Saxon architecture in Hampshire.

The original church was considerably larger; it is probable that the narthex or baptistery at the west end, and a north porticus*, were both demolished in the 15th century. The tower was also higher, the upper wooden sections having long since gone, and the chancel was once the same height as the nave.

The long-and-short stonework at the corners of the tower and of the south porticus is typical of the period. Several Saxon windows remain although some can be seen only from the inside while others have been blocked or replaced. Internally, the 15th-century arches between nave, tower and chancel are replacements for Saxon ones, which would have been similar to that between tower and south porticus *(see page 22)*.

Until the major restoration of 1897 the exterior was covered in coats of plaster which obscured the flintwork. The roof of the 12th-century south porch was raised in the early 16th century to form a small chapel around the Saxon rood (a bas-relief of the crucifixion). The rood was probably moved here from the demolished western chamber. Sadly, the rood was defaced during the religious upheavals of the Reformation.

*A 'porticus' is similar to a transept, but is distinguished by not being of the same width as the tower. The south porticus is now used as the vestry.

The Church is generally open to visitors throughout the year when there are no services in progress.
A more detailed Guide Book (by the present authors) and picture postcards are available in the church.

The most remarkable feature of the church is a narrow Saxon arch *(left above)* which survives between the tower and the south porticus. It retains its original inscription 'HER SWUTELATH SEO GECWYDRAEDNES THE', which translates as 'Here is made plain the covenant to Thee'.

The churchyard yew tree *(left below)* may be one of the oldest surviving features of the village - it was probably already a mature tree at the time the church was built.

The appointment of priests was in the gift of the Priors of Breamore in the Middle Ages. At the time of the Reformation, the church's dedication was changed from St Michael to St Mary. From then until recently, the village's 'rector' was actually a curate nominated by the Lay Rector – a position generally held by the Lord of the Manor. As the parish is now part of the Avon Valley Team Partnership based in Fordingbridge, Breamore no longer has its own resident incumbent.

From the church, walk back through the car-park of the Countryside Museum. On reaching a lane, turn right, then left and walk along Upper Street with its thatched cottages. Behind a high wall on the right is a larger house – the Rookery.

THE ROOKERY

This large 17th-century house in Upper Street takes its name from the Rooke family who built it. There are records of the family in Breamore from the 15th century. By the 18th century they had become gentlemen farmers and the Rookes were one of the most important families in the village.

Just past the Rookery is a staggered junction with large trees in the centre, known as 'Cross Trees'.
A short detour to the right here, along Rookery Lane, leads to a fine staddle stone barn (see page 47).
Upper Street continues ahead and leads after half-a-mile to the hamlet of Outwick (see page 46).
However, to continue the tour, turn left down Fry's Hill. At the bottom of the hill you reach the large open area of Breamore Marsh. There are a number of thatched cottages to be admired around the edge of the Marsh.

23

THE MARSH

Although the forty-acre area of grassland known as the Marsh is not registered as common land today, it has nevertheless been used to pasture grazing animals belonging to tenants of Breamore Estate for centuries. The earliest record is from 1298 when 36 sheep were kept there for a total payment of 6d (2½p). Freeholders and their sub-tenants, the Lord of the Manor, the rector and the miller were specifically excluded from using this grazing.

In 1647 the manor court stipulated that no tenants were to *'suffer their sheep to depasture in the Marsh of Breamore at any time of the year, save only the 24th day of December until the Sunday after Candlemas (Feb 2nd) upon pain of 2d for every 24 hours that they shall depasture there'*.

Geese have also been grazed on the Marsh since at least the 15th century. In 1585 two tenants were fined 6d each for overstocking the pasture with their geese. In 18th-century court papers it was regularly ordered that *'no tenant was to keep more than two geese and one gander on the Marsh from 25th December until 25th March on pain of 3d for every*

A view looking towards Marshlands *(see p.28)* with Breamore's remaining flock of geese

extra goose or gander'. However the two geese would normally hatch a large clutch of goslings around the end of March – providing roast goose for Christmas!

Cattle and geese may still be seen on the Marsh, although in much smaller numbers than previously. The grazing has always been controlled by a manorial official, the Hayward, and this honorary post is still filled by one of the Estate tenants. The Marsh, with its stream and ponds (Long Pond, Round Pond and Mitchell's Pond), is a designated Site of Special Scientific Interest, largely due to the presence of several rare and obscure plants.

The Marsh has also been used as the village sports ground for very many years. Cricket and football were being played here during Victorian times, with the former recorded as early as 1833. The football club was in existence in 1875, with Fordingbridge being their first reported opponents on January 2nd. Breamore won 5–0. Sadly, there is no longer a Breamore football team, but village cricket still thrives. The unusual thatched, flint-built cricket pavilion dates from the early years of the 20th century. It was used as the HQ of the village Home Guard during the Second World War.

TOP - Long Pond in the 1920s
MIDDLE - Breamore's successful
football team of the 1920-21 season
(goal aggregate for 17 matches: 90-8)
BOTTOM - the cricket pavilion today

View across
Round Pond
towards the
bottom of
Fry's Hill

This cottage
housed the
village school-
room from
around 1830
till 1872 *(see
page 40)*

THATCHED COTTAGES

The many picturesque thatched cottages which survive in Breamore are one of the delights of the village. Most date from between 1600 and 1650, but some incorporate earlier work, mostly from the later years of the previous century. Part of one cottage in Upper Street incorporates the timber frame of the 15th-century cottage that previously stood on the site.

Indeed, most of the cottages are on the sites of earlier ones which can now be traced only in the archives. Almost all began life as farmhouses or the dwellings of smallholders, some of whom were engaged in crafts such as smithing or carpentry. At various times, some of the cottages were pressed into service as alehouses, inns, shops, a parish poor-house, post-offices and even the original school.

The rapidly increasing population of the 18th and 19th centuries led to cottages being divided up to form small households for farmworkers. Since the late 1950s, a number of estate cottages have passed into private ownership. In the subsequent modernisations, several cottages were often combined (or re-combined) into single dwellings. The tenanted cottages were modernised in the 1980s, with 20th-century conveniences reaching some Breamore inhabitants quite late in the century!

The higher right-hand section of this cottage in Upper Street, in common with many thatched cottages in Breamore, dates from the early 17th century. The lower left-hand section, however, is a surviving part of a much older cottage. (Photographed 1980)

Continue along the lane, with the Marsh and Round Pond on your right. You pass several interesting cottages on your left. (Please see note on respecting privacy on page 4.)

CLOCKWISE FROM TOP LEFT:

the Lodge House (1898);

'Marshlands' clearly housed three families at this time (1898);

pair of Victorian cottages (2005);

Dodington House (2005).

THE NORTHERN EDGE OF THE MARSH

In the angle of Fry's Hill and Wally Hill (an alternative route back to Breamore House), stands a Victorian **Lodge House**. Records show that this was built in 1890 at a total cost of £220. This included £70 for stone and £35 for bricks. Several features, including the chimneys and windows, were inspired by the Tudor architecture of Breamore House.

A little further along, beyond a thatched cottage set back from the road, is the '**Reading Room**', or former village 'library'. A plaque over the door of this flint cottage (now a private dwelling) records that it was built in 1901 in memory of Charles Hulse who was killed in action during the Boer War.

A large thatched cottage on the left (**'Marshlands'**) has an incongruous bay-window, which dates from its spell as a shop during the late 19th and early 20th centuries. Nearby, there is a pair of **Victorian cottages**, rebuilt after a fire in 1886. These cottages again show the inspiration of Breamore House.

Partly hidden by trees near the north-east corner of the Marsh stands **Dodington House**. This was the site of one of the Priory's farms and tithe barn before the Dissolution. A rectory was established here during the 16th century. It was entirely rebuilt by Sir William Dodington in the 1630s, and largely replaced again by the Reverend May in 1804. Its present name was chosen when it ceased to be the village rectory and was sold as a private dwelling in the 1950s.

The rectangular flint building nearby was originally the Rectory **dovecot**, but has long been converted into a house.

Dodington Cottage, the former Rectory dovecot

Leaving the Marsh, the lane reaches the main road, with the Hulse Hall immediately opposite.

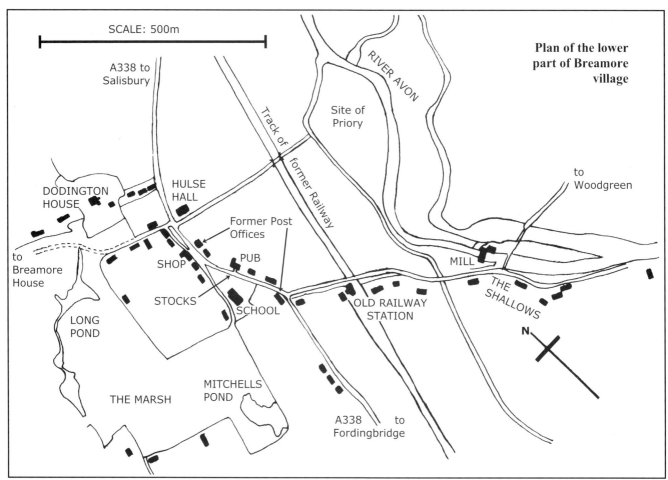

SCALE: 500m

Plan of the lower part of Breamore village

A338 to Salisbury

RIVER AVON

Track of former Railway

Site of Priory

to Woodgreen

DODINGTON HOUSE

HULSE HALL

Former Post Offices

to Breamore House

SHOP

PUB

MILL

THE SHALLOWS

STOCKS

SCHOOL

OLD RAILWAY STATION

N

LONG POND

THE MARSH

MITCHELLS POND

A338 to Fordingbridge

THE HULSE HALL

The Hulse Hall was given to the village in June 1927 by Lady Hulse. It has been in regular use ever since for concerts, plays, sales of work, flower shows and many other local events.

In medieval times, a wayfarers' chapel dedicated to St Thomas stood just across the road from this spot.

RIGHT: interior of the hall - a Mothers' Union Sale of work in aid of church funds in about 1935
BELOW: the Hall in 2005

The track to the right of the Hall leads down into the riverside meadow where Breamore Priory once stood (see pages 32-33). There is little to see in the meadow today – and in any case, there is NO public right of way on this track. So, leaving the area of the Hulse Hall, go south along the lane which closely parallels the main A338 Salisbury-Ringwood road. The former village shop is on the right, with the former post office opposite (see pages 34-37).

Seal of Breamore Priory
showing St Michael, 1478

THE PRIORY

The Augustinian Priory of St. Michael was founded in about 1130 A.D. by Baldwin de Redvers, Lord of the Manor of Breamore, and later Earl of Devon. The Priory's extensive lands within Breamore were gradually extended, mainly in the form of many small gifts in return for prayers offered up by the Canons. By 1350 it owned almost half of the lands and houses in the village and many other properties as far afield as Dorset, Somerset and Devon. The Priory let much of its land to tenants, but the Canons and Lay Brothers farmed several hundred acres of arable, pasture and meadow themselves. They also grazed about 300 sheep on the downs. The Priory was thus self-sufficient in many basic foodstuffs and is known to have produced wool for sale in the 14th century at least.

As the 14th and 15th centuries progressed, economic circumstances changed. Almost all the monastic land was let to tenant farmers; the wealth of the Priory declined. It suffered severe flooding of its riverside site in the 1470s and could ill afford to repair the extensive damage. Before the end of the century the Prior and Canons had debts of £650, while by the 1530s the Priory House and outbuildings were said to be in 'ruyn and decaye'.

The Dissolution of the Priory, on the orders of Henry VIII's commissioners, took place on 5th July 1536. One of the Canons, Edward Cadwell, soon became Vicar of Whitsbury; the last Prior, James Finch, was given a pension and two years later was appointed Suffragan Bishop of Taunton; the remaining six Canons returned to secular life and disappeared from the records.

A model created by one of the authors (AL) to give an impression of the Priory buildings adjacent to the River Avon

By the early 17th century all the buildings had been demolished. Many local cottages of that date contain small quantities of worked stone removed from the rubble *(see picture, page 8)*. As late as the 1760s, many hundreds of cart-loads of stone were being dug up and removed from the foundations. Today only low banks and ditches remain at the site. Study of these earth-works reveals that the plan of the Priory was typical of Augustinian establishments, with the church north of the cloister, and with other buildings arranged around it.

The only remnants of the priory to be seen by the visitor are a few tiles on display in Breamore House and three stone coffins which now lie under the yew tree in Breamore churchyard. Both the tiles and the coffins were found during excavations in 1898.

RIGHT: The cottage, opposite the road to Woodgreen, which housed the Post Office from 1870 till 1914 - now known as the Old Post Office

FACING PAGE: the purpose-built Post Office used from 1914 till 1981 - now known as the Post House

Members of the Duell family and their staff appear in both pictures on these old postcards

Post Office, Breamore.

POST OFFICES

Although there was no post office in the village at that time, it is on record that in 1867 letters were received by John Edsall, the schoolmaster, at 5.30 a.m. Deliveries around the village began half an hour later. Outgoing post was dispatched by John Edsall at 7.45 each evening. There was a telegraph office at the railway station, but the nearest money order office was in Fordingbridge.

In 1870 John Edsall emigrated to Canada and it was then that a cottage opposite the turning to Woodgreen was converted into a Post Office by the new sub-postmaster, Henry Duell. By 1899 there were two deliveries a day and one on Sundays, not only within Breamore, but also

Post Office, Breamore.

A copy of this postcard sent on 21st December 1914 carried this message:

'P.O. Breamore, Salisbury, Wilts. ...... good wishes for Xmas and the New Year. This is our new house; we have been in it for 4 months now. I have a very nice office & much more room & more convenient. I am in the doorway, with Father & my brother on either side of me. Two of our friends at the gate & Amy standing near the pram, with my sister Cissie's youngest child in it, he is now nine months old & a fine child. ...... Patty Duell.'

for Charford, Woodgreen and Whitsbury. At this time and for some years afterwards – until the introduction of bicycles – all deliveries were made on foot. When delivering to Whitsbury, the postman had a round trip of about five miles.

The building shown above was constructed as a purpose-built Post Office in 1914. Since 1981, it has been a private dwelling known as the Post House; the cottage used before 1914 had already been named 'the Old Post Office'. Today all deliveries are from vans based in Fordingbridge.

The Old Pine Stores today. The attached dwelling is now named Kilford House after a former village shopkeeper.

THE VILLAGE SHOP

The Old Pine Stores opened in 2003 in the premises of the former Breamore Stores. There had been a shop selling groceries and provisions on this site since at least the 1860s when it was owned by John Hall.

The existing building incorporates some older parts, but largely dates from 1895 when it was rebuilt by James Kilford, a local baker and grocer. He sold the shop a few years later to Thomas Vince. Before the days of delivery vans, bread and groceries were taken many miles by horse and cart.

Bread was baked on the premises until the late 1950s when the shop was owned by Bert Candy. 'Candy's' also operated a mobile shop around the nearby villages, with most homes visited twice a week. The delivery service ended, the victim of competition from supermarkets, when the last van driver, George Roberts, retired in 1989. He had completed over 50 years service, having started on a bicycle with a side-cart.

In 1981 the village Post Office was incorporated into the shop, following closure of the premises opposite. Since the winding up of Breamore Stores, there has been no post office in the village.

Prior to 1860, Breamore, like many other villages, would have had craftsmen selling goods, usually the product of their own labours, from workshops in their own cottages. They included such trades as tailors, carpenters and shoemakers. Provisions and goods which were not produced locally could be obtained from hawkers or by travelling to markets, fairs and shops in nearby towns. Most people grew their own vegetables and perhaps fruit, while smallholders and farmers were usually willing to sell spare produce to those who had no land.

Thus, historically, village shops are a fairly recent development. Not surprisingly, the first shops in Breamore opened at about the time of the arrival of the railway, which enabled goods to be delivered relatively cheaply from the larger towns.

A little further south along the main road is the village pub, the Bat and Ball.

Two versions of *The Boy with the Bat* used as inn-signs for Breamore's pub. The lower one dates from late 2003; the upper one had been in place for some years prior to this date.

THE BAT AND BALL

The Bat and Ball was opened by William Pearce soon after 1830. It took its name from the cricket played nearby on the Marsh. The modern inn-sign shows an 18th-century cricketer, and was inspired by *The Boy with the Bat*. The original painting may be seen in Breamore House; it shows only two stumps as it was painted before the introduction of the third. The Bat and Ball was the successor of another inn, the Wellington Arms, which had recently closed following the death of its owner.

There must have been earlier inns here, but none is recorded by name. However, many different houses in the village have operated as alehouses at one time or another. In the 15th century, up to twenty Breamore smallholders regularly brewed ale for sale. Most villages had

FACING PAGE: The original thatched Bat and Ball - a photograph dating from about 1890

LEFT: the present-day pub, in a building which dates from the early years of the 20th century

similar numbers of brewers at the time. Anyone who brewed was visited regularly by 'aletasters', elected manorial officials, whose task it was to check that the regulations relating to the sale of liquor were being adhered to. As late as 1841 William Sutton was keeping a beer shop in a cottage on the north side of the Marsh.

Today the Bat and Ball, refurbished in 2003, attracts the custom of locals and visitors alike. Situated alongside the busy A338, it benefits from a great deal of passing trade, particularly in the summer months.

Opposite the pub are the grounds of the village school (pages 40-41). Set in the hedge surrounding the school are the village stocks (page 42)

Two early photographs of Breamore School

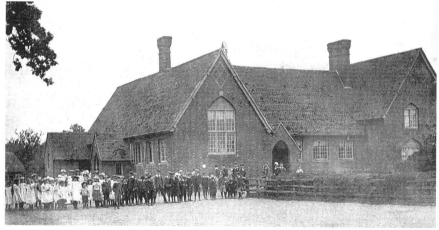

THE VILLAGE SCHOOL

Breamore Church of England School was built in 1872, and was designed for an intended maximum of 160 children. The building included an adjoining house for the head-teacher.

Formal education in the village began around 1830, when James Froud was recorded as Breamore's first schoolmaster. (Only three years earlier, he had been a labourer at Woodgreen.) He was assisted by two elderly spinsters, Mary and Ann Davage, in a schoolroom established in a thatched cottage on the Marsh, at the foot of Fry's Hill *(see page 26)*.

In the early years there were only classes for infants and boys, but by 1837 there were 58 boys and 48 girls attending the school, with 110 at the Sunday School. In 1851 the master was John Edsall, son of the local blacksmith, and there was a staff of four. In 1870 John emigrated to Thamesville, Ontario, where he quickly became church organist and Superintendent of Sunday Schools. He was succeeded in Breamore by Henry Sinden, who oversaw the move to the new purpose-built premises.

Breamore School, 2005, showing the modern extensions

For many years, it was an Elementary School, with pupils continuing their education till the official school-leaving age. In 1956, when secondary-education-for-all came late to the area with the opening of The Burgate School, the age range at Breamore was reduced to 5–11 year-olds. The school garden, where older boys had been taught gardening, was replaced by a tarmac playground.

Today Breamore Primary School is thriving and successful. Extensions were built in the 1990s and, most recently, the former teacher's house was converted to provide extra space. In 2005 there were 131 pupils from Breamore and surrounding villages and a teaching staff of seven.

After viewing the stocks (page 42) and the school from the main road, one may take the narrow lane on the other side of the school grounds. After a short distance, the school is on your left and a cottage called Marsh Holding (the former Wellington Arms) is on your right. School Lane leads directly onto the Marsh. At this point, it is easy to return to the starting point at the Countryside Museum by crossing the Marsh on footpaths to the Lodge House and taking Wally Hill, signposted to Breamore House. However, taking great care with the traffic, the old railway station and the former mill may be included in this 'tour' of the village by crossing the main road and walking along the lane towards Woodgreen.

THE VILLAGE STOCKS

As in most villages, the stocks were a form of punishment from medieval times until the mid-19th century. Those in Breamore were doubtless used on many occasions, but only one actual record seems to have survived: on 17th February 1586 John Cooke was *'whipped at the post'* and then put into the stocks for three hours. His crime had been the theft of a white horse belonging to John Harris.

Breamore is fortunate to have had its ancient stocks preserved. Even after they were no longer needed they were kept in repair by the local carpenter, and are today near their original position on Little Marsh. Most of this green disappeared when the school was built, and the stocks were enclosed within its gardens. Following road widening, they now stand on the roadside. The roof is a relatively modern attempt to provide some protection from the weather.

For continuation of the walk, see note on the previous page.

THE RAILWAY STATION

The railway line from Salisbury to Wimborne, passing through Breamore, was closed in May 1963. Over forty years later the derelict station building still stands.

It was in 1861 that plans for the line were first proposed, but almost three years elapsed before there was sufficient finance available to begin. The work started in April 1864 and was completed during the autumn of 1865. Numerous delays had been caused principally by a dispute over the siting of Fordingbridge station, and by problems with bridge construction. The first trains ran on Thursday 20th December 1865. Originally it was envisaged that the line would be extended to a double track, but financial problems prevented this ever happening.

At first only a goods siding was proposed for Breamore, but the plans were soon amended and a station was built in time for the opening of the line. In the early years there were four trains a day in each direction, the return third class fare to Fordingbridge being 5d (2p) and that to Salisbury 1s 10d (9p).

TOP: Don and Bert Young, with station master Cliff Young, on the 'up' platform at Breamore
LOWER PICTURE: The derelict station in 2005
INSERT: a rare postcard of the Breamore signal box

BREAMORE MILL AND THE MEADOWS

The picturesque mill buildings which survive today are largely of 18th- and 19th-century date, but a mill has existed here for over eight centuries. It was established by the nearby Priory in the 12th century and remained monastic property until 1536, after which it was incorporated into the Breamore Estate.

In the Middle Ages the mill was owned by the Priory and leased by it to successive millers. Anyone from the village having their grain ground here had to pay a fee; this was usually a proportion of the flour produced. Here, as elsewhere, millers were very unpopular, often being accused of keeping too much of the flour or meal.

A print of Breamore Mill from 1792 by J. Sigrist - see also back cover

The earliest known miller was Ralph Berkham, recorded in 1480. The names of many of his successors are known, ending with Stanley Hall who retired in 1970. In the last few decades of activity, the mill machinery was used to manufacture animal feeding stuffs, which were delivered to farmers and smallholders in the villages around by horse and wagon.

The former wide expanse of water below the Mill led to the name of The Shallows being used for the small group of cottages here. In earlier times, when most of the cottages were owned by the Priory, the locality had been known as Milton.

The shallows themselves were crossed by a ford until construction of the brick bridge in 1867. However, pedestrians and horses could cross the millstream on a wooden bridge from the 16th century; the present iron bridge was built in about 1900.

Between the Mill and Charford, much of the flood plain of the River Avon was managed as watermeadows from the mid-17th century until the 1950s. A complex system of ditches and hatches was used to irrigate the land in December, producing an early crop of grass. In this way, early grazing was available, or two crops of hay could be produced in each year. As the grassland was 'unimproved' it was full of the typical wild flowers of meadowland.

Breamore's two bridges over the River Avon

This ends the 'walking tour'. However, as Breamore is a scattered village, we have also included sections on the hamlet of Outwick (page 46) and a number of outlying farms (page 47).

OUTWICK

The tiny hamlet of Outwick, to the south of Upper Street, has an interesting history. Archaeological fieldwork has shown that there was late Iron Age habitation a little to the west of the present hamlet and that this was succeeded by a Romano-British settlement on an adjacent site. Outwick was mentioned in the Domesday Survey of 1086 as Otoiche; at that time, it was owned by Waleran the Huntsman and sub-let to Gozelin. It continued to be held separately from Breamore until it was incorporated into the Estate in 1743.

The medieval cottages were mostly along the track that leads to the woods, although there was one further to the west which may have been associated with the local tile-making industry. In more recent times the clay here has been used for brick making and some evidence of 19th- and early-20th-century kilns can still be seen.

The hamlet has never been large, but it has varied in size from time to time. Mostly, there seem to have been about six cottages, but during the 19th century the population expanded considerably. By the time of the 1851 census the houses were divided into sixteen households with a total of 81 inhabitants.

Outwick, photographed by James Coventry of Burgate House in the 1890s
(Courtesy Hampshire Record Office)

FARMS AND BARNS

Breamore has a number of farmsteads, each with its own history. For example, **Roundhill Farm**, between Outwick and Whitsbury, was originally a grange or monastic farm attached to the Priory. Lay brothers, assisted by hired workmen, grew corn on the arable land and tended the Priory's flock of over 300 sheep, grazing on Breamore Down. By the 15th century, the farm was leased to tenant farmers. In later times it has been one of the main farms in the parish. The existing thatched farmhouse dates from the 17th century, and is now a private dwelling. Others, such as North Street Farm, Down Farm and Flood Street Farm, have long ceased to be working farms.

William Dodington established a farm on the edge of Breamore Park in the 1580s. For many years it was known simply as 'The Barns'. One barn was converted into a farmhouse in about 1790. The farm was intended as the **Home Farm** of the Estate, although at times it was let out to tenant farmers, particularly towards the end of the 17th century and in the late 1700s.

The largest barn, on the west side, still exists in its original form; a few years ago it was fully restored and re-roofed, using old tiles. During the restoration, an unique ridge tile was found, bearing the remnants of a figure of a cow *(right)*. An adjacent barn, still standing on staddle stones in order to protect the contents from vermin, is one of a number surviving in the village. A fine example, of 19th-century date, may be seen in Rookery Lane.

TOP: staddle stone barn at Roundhill, 1898
CENTRE: barns at Flood Street Farm, 1898
BOTTOM: 16th-century roof tile from the
Home Farm barn

Other publications on Breamore village

A Walk to Breamore Miz-maze (2nd ed.) by Anthony Light and Gerald Ponting, 2000, ISBN 0953395502
A Coin Hoard from Roman Breamore by Anthony Light and Gerald Ponting, 2001, ISBN 0953395510
The Saxon Church of St Mary's, Breamore by Anthony Light and Gerald Ponting, 2004, ISBN 0953395545
Scenes from a Hampshire Childhood by Gerald Ponting, 2004, ISBN 0951742361
Breamore House and Countryside Museum (official guide book)

  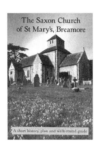 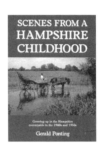 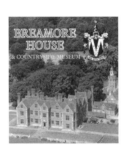

Acknowledgements

The authors wish to thank the following for their assistance in compiling this book:

Sir Edward Hulse of Breamore House (10th Baronet) for his assistance in many ways, including permission to include the photograph of the coin hoard on page 6, the print on page 12, the paintings on pages 15 and 17, the print on page 44 and the back cover, and all the photographs captioned '1898' which were taken from a Hulse family photo-album;

Thomas Ross Collection and Intaglio Fine Art for permission to use the print of Green's Farm on the cover and page 3;

Winchester Museums Service for use of the photograph of the bronze 'bucket' on page 6;

on page 7 the text from Domesday Book is reproduced, by kind permission, from the Phillimore edition (General Editor, John Morris) volume 4, Hampshire, published 1982 by Phillimore and Co Ltd, Shopwycke Manor Barn, Chichester, PO20 2BG;

the *Salisbury Journal* for permission to include the aerial view of the Miz-Maze on page 19;

Hampshire Record Office for use of the Outwick photograph on page 46.

Our thanks also to our wives, Elizabeth Light and Elizabeth Ponting, for their support in many ways; to Barbara Burbridge for her efficient proof reading; and to Hobbs the Printers for their usual excellent service.